F.I.G.H.T.
From Not Enough To Good Enough

DAMION S. HUTCHINS

Copyright © 2018 Damion S. Hutchins

All rights reserved. No part of this book may be used or reproduced by any means, graphic, electronic or mechanical, including photocopying, recording, taping or by any information storage retrieval system without the written permission of the author except in the case of brief quotations embodied in critical articles and reviews.

Printed in the United States of America.

CreateSpace, Charleston, SC

ISBN: 1979962022
ISBN-13: 978-1979962025

DEDICATION

In memory of my big sister, Latoya Dokes.
Thank you for believing in me even when I didn't believe in me!
I love you and dearly miss you!
(1974–2005)

TABLE OF CONTENTS

ACKNOWLEDGMENTS 7
PREFACE 9
1 WHO ME? NAH. 13
2 FAITH 23
    Faith in God 25
    Faith in yourself 26
    Faith in your destiny 27
    Faith in your failure 30
3 IMAGINATION 35
    You can't achieve what you don't imagine! 37
    Imagination is specific to you! 38
    Imagination is not coincidental! 39
    Imagination is dynamic! 40
4 GOALS 45
    Enter your destination 47
    Watch out for distractions 50
    Recalculating 52
    You have arrived at your destination 54
5 HELP 57
    The pride complex 59
    "I got it! Or so I thought!" 62
    Blocked blessings 65
6 TIME 71
    Patience 73

Stop and smell the roses 74
The butterfly effect 76
Time to soar 78

7 LOVE LIFTED ME 83
What love is not 85
Love pains 88
Love looks like you 89

8 GET OUT OF YOUR WAY! 93
Procrastination 94
Negative self-talk 97
Comparing apples to oranges 100

ABOUT THE AUTHOR 105

ACKNOWLEDGMENTS

First, to the Creator who thought enough of me to give me life and to gift me with a passion and a purpose, I am eternally grateful.

To my wife Williemae, who continued to encourage me to write even when I didn't think it would be worth the time, thank you for staying on me. We finally did it! I love you! (Now it's YOUR turn!)

To my daughter Jada, "Daddy's Lil' Nugget," thank you for teaching me the importance of appreciating the beauty in every moment. May you always know that YOU ARE GOOD ENOUGH! Nothing will be able to stop you when you put your best foot forward! Daddy loves you!

To the rest of my family, whether biological, adoptive, or fictive, thank you for the role you've played in my life. You all have helped me to become the man I am today. For you I am grateful.

To my close friends, you all know who you are! Thank you for believing in me and for continuing to keep me on my timeline! Thank you for letting me vent and process "life" with you all as I was working through how to write this book. I love you all to life!

To Kerry, my therapist, I finally listened and took some of your excellent advice! Thank you so much!

To my colleagues in chaplaincy and in pastoral ministry, thank you for the privilege of serving alongside you! Many of you are already authors and you have all inspired me to tell my story.

To O'Nae, my writing coach, thank you for inspiring me in more ways than one! Keep encouraging people to follow their dreams and to live their authentic truth!

To Cynthia, my editor, thank you for hard work and phenomenal recommendations!

To all of the churches I have served, and the many pastors who have mentored me along the way, THANK YOU!

No matter who you are or how we are connected, know that I appreciate you ALL! This book is for YOU!

PREFACE

Thank you for reading my book. This is my first attempt at trying to articulate in writing my journey from a place of low self-esteem and diminished self-worth to a place of confidence and courage. This book has been years in the making. In some ways, I feel like that was part of the plan all along. I needed to experience some of the more difficult parts of my journey in order to fully appreciate the tools and tips that I will offer to you in this book.

I struggled with the title of this book for so long because it seems to go against everything I believe as an inspiring, encouraging, compassionate individual. Typically, people like me are not fighters. But as this manuscript was taking shape, I realized that life can be a fight, especially for those of us who have struggled for years with the feeling that we were never good enough. Not only is it a fight to live through every day, it is an even greater fight to overcome.

F.I.G.H.T. is an acronym for faith, imagination, goals, help, and time. These are the foundational tools that have helped me to overcome years of depression and feeling worthless. In the chapter on faith, I explain how I view the concept of faith and the way it can help us to better appreciate both the good and bad parts of our journey. In the chapter on imagination, I share how the ideas and visions we have for our life are given to us specifically for a purpose. No one else has been given our assignment. It is up to us to determine what we will do with it.

Goals are designed to help keep us on track in accomplishing our vision. My hope is that using the image of a GPS system will be a helpful analogy for better understanding how to map out our journey toward becoming good enough. Help is the next tool in this equation. No person is an island. We don't get to our lowest places in life alone; therefore, it is highly unlikely that we will be able to emerge from those places without the assistance of others. Finally, since rebuilding (emotionally or otherwise) does not happen overnight, it will take time and patience to see maximum results. Using the image of the caterpillar's transition to a butterfly was a helpful way for me to describe this process in that chapter.

I've added a few additional chapters to the end of the F.I.G.H.T. model because I've found these additional tips to be helpful in my personal process. Love has helped me to better understand myself and see others as valuable. It is an often-misunderstood concept, however, and should not be lightly handled. I became aware of ways in which I was self-sabotaging my own success. I had to quickly learn how to get out of my own way so that I would not cause myself more harm.

At the end of each chapter, I have offered some questions to ponder. The purpose of these questions is to get you thinking more deeply about the information in the chapter and ways in which you can apply the information to your life. These questions may also be helpful as you share this book with others in small groups or just around the water cooler. This is just another way to get us talking about issues that you may discover are not just unique to me and you.

While I am a Christian pastor and chaplain by calling and education, I have been intentional about not making this a "Scripture heavy" book. My intention is to tell my story from a place of authenticity without preaching to others what they should or should not do "according to the Bible." I have made a couple of Scripture references that particularly resonate with my journey, but it felt more true to share my story using primarily my own words. I hope this book will make you laugh, reflect, and ultimately take action as you move from not enough to GOOD ENOUGH.

1
WHO ME? NAH.

"And suddenly you know: it's time to start something new and trust the magic of beginnings."
~Meister Eckhart

Simone sat in my office with tears in her eyes. For the past hour, we had been talking about how she felt trapped in a dead-end job and had been considering a change in career fields. She was considering becoming a certified nursing assistant (CNA) or a patient care technician. As I sat there listening to her talk, her voice lacked excitement and passion; her body language and her tone of voice conveyed boredom and disinterest. Yes, the career change would likely have earned her more money, but there was clearly no joy in her expression; in fact, there was little expression at all. Intuitively, I asked,

"What is it that you *really* want to do with your life?" She looked at me as if, at worst, I had just asked her a trick question. At best, perhaps I was giving her permission to be authentic, honest, and real.

Simone carefully considered her response for a moment, and then a big smile came on her face. She said, "Well, to be honest, I've really always wanted to be a nurse!" She paused for a moment as if waiting for me to affirm or reject her response. "Yes, a nurse! That's what I really want to be," she continued. I responded, "Then why are we talking about all these other careers? If you want to be a nurse, then let's work on you becoming a nurse! Stop shooting for less than what you really want!" Suddenly, as quickly as her smile had appeared, it was gone. Simone's response was confusing for me; it was as if I had taken all the air out of her newly blown-up balloon. She continued, "But you don't understand! I'm not smart enough to be a nurse. I would never get into nursing school. I've never been great in English and Math. No, I'm just not smart enough to be a nurse. So I guess I'll just be a CNA."

As I watched and listened to Simone talk herself out of pursuing her own dream, it made me think about my own dreams. I couldn't fault her, because I have talked myself out of what I really want to do for years! I could relate to Simone's story so well because I've often struggled with feeling that I wasn't "good enough" to do one thing or another. In fact, if the truth be told, it's amazing that you're reading this book! For years, I've had the dream of becoming an author, but I kept saying to myself, "Damion, you're not a good writer! You're not smart enough to write a book. What makes you think anyone would even read your book?" This self-defeating attitude did not just start with writing a book; for most of my life, I've struggled with whether I could accomplish any of my dreams.

When I was about seven years old, I learned that I was adopted as a young child. It wasn't until I was well into my 20s that I learned the story of how I came to be and the circumstances which led to my adoption. I was the third child born to a 19-year-old mother in Akron, Ohio. According to my adoption records, my mother had a history of drug addiction and prostitution. By the time I was born, my older brother and sister had already been taken away from my mother and were in foster care or had been adopted by the State. When I was six months old, my mother left me with a great aunt to care for me while she went off to do "who knows what." My aunt was frustrated with my mother for "always leaving her kids" and called social services to have me taken into state custody; she felt that my mother had essentially abandoned me.

Over the next few years, I was shuttled from foster home to foster home. When I was four years old, I was adopted by a married couple in Cleveland, Ohio. Not long after I was adopted, they divorced, and I was raised (eventually along with my three brothers) by my adoptive mother. One day I will write a book about my life with her and my brothers, but for now, suffice it to say that those were some very challenging years in my life. When I was fourteen years old, I went to live with my adoptive father and his wife.

In hindsight, making that transition felt like "jumping from the frying pan into the fire." The two years I lived with them were some of the toughest years of my life. On the one hand, I lived with an adoptive father who had been absent practically most of my life. He didn't know me; therefore it was very difficult for me to believe he could possibly love me, especially while he was beating me for something he was told that I had done wrong without having any proof. His wife was, hmm, how do I say this nicely? She was the epitome of the "evil stepmother." I never understood why she seemed to have a problem with everything I did, but her own two children could get away with highway robbery and murder with a get-out-of-jail-free pass. Most of my memories living with them are unpleasant. But what stands out most is their regular reminders that I was adopted. I remember them telling me that I would probably end up "in the system" just like the rest of my family members. I remember them telling me that I was likely not going to amount to much. "You're never going to be good enough to be anything worthwhile," they said. And I believed it. For a long, long time, I believed it.

Today I can proudly say that I'm no longer a prisoner to their prophecies! But that experience also taught me a valuable lesson: words have power! Whoever came up with the expression, "Sticks and stones may break my bones, but words will never hurt me," was sadly mistaken. This is why I am so careful when I talk to my own daughter. No matter what she has done or how frustrated I may become with her behavior, there is no reason to demean or berate her or make her feel like she is less than the beautifully created being of God that she is. This is not only true for my daughter, but it extends to the way I treat people in general. Speak positive words to people; it truly makes a difference!

In 1998, I started searching for my biological family, and I was blessed to be reunited with them in 2003. Within the same week of April 2003, I was united with my older brother, older sister, and two younger sisters. My two youngest sisters had been adopted together within our biological family. But, of the five of us, Latoya (my older sister) and I developed the closest bond. However, she was ill when we met. She died almost two years later at the age of 30 from complications of lupus. Before she died, we talked almost every day on the telephone, sometimes multiple times a day. We talked about our lives and the challenges we've overcome, and she would ask me, "When are you going to write your book?" I always jokingly responded, "Who me? Nah." Latoya was one of my biggest cheerleaders and she always believed that I could do far more than I believed. We all need a Latoya in our lives!

I only knew my sister Latoya for about two years, but she made an indelible impression on my life and my future, perhaps without even realizing it. You can do the same for people with your words of encouragement, optimism, and the way in which you offer your unconditional support! Be for others what you would like others to be for you!

At the time, I didn't realize that most of my hesitation about becoming an author (or realizing any of my other dreams) was motivated by fear: fear of success, fear of failure, fear of haters, fear of facing my past, etc. Yet it is that same fear which has propelled me to action. The day I had that conversation with Simone, I said to myself, "Fear will no longer overtake me. I'm tired of being afraid! I can do this! I AM GOOD ENOUGH!" There, I said it! I AM GOOD ENOUGH! And guess what? YOU ARE GOOD ENOUGH TOO!

But saying, affirming, and putting that "good enough" belief into practice are three different things! It's not until you activate what you say you believe about yourself that you will see your dreams come to pass. Only when you move from merely *saying* "I AM GOOD ENOUGH" to doing things that prove (to yourself and the world) that you ARE will you be able to overcome the walls of fear and doubt that seem to be the foundational stumbling blocks that keep you from moving forward. If I can do it, you can too! That's why I'm writing this book!

When I was preparing to write this book, my writing coach said, "Give me three reasons why you've decided to write this book *now*." Without giving it much thought, I responded. "First, I'm writing this book so I can stop lying to myself!" Most of my friends are published authors. I've been to their book signings. I've purchased their books. I've recommended their books to others. But when my friends asked, "So, Damion, when are you going to write your book?" I often responded, "Who me? Nah. That's your thing. You know I'm a storyteller, not a writer."

The truth was that no matter how often I told my author friends that I *didn't* want to write a book, inside I knew that I really *DID* want to write a book. I *did* want my friends and colleagues to be as proud of me as I have been of them over the years. I *did* want people to celebrate my first book and start encouraging me to write my second and third. But I was too ashamed and embarrassed to admit that I didn't feel confident enough to do it! One of the things I am learning is that our words and thoughts have power. When I started to say and believe that people would read my book and that I could be a successful author, it was amazing how smoothly the process started to become. *(By the way, thank you for reading my book; you are proving my point!)*

The second reason for writing this book now is that "I *have* to do this!" For me, procrastination was no longer an option. As a pastor, chaplain, and motivational speaker, I spend almost every moment of every day inspiring and encouraging others: "Reach for the stars! Follow your dreams! Don't let anything stop you!" But when it came to taking my own advice, that little voice in my head would often say, "Yeah, but that's not really advice for me; that's for them" or "Well, maybe I'll start tomorrow." Listen, I've been "starting tomorrow" for the past twenty years! It won't be too long before life will have passed me by. I don't want to be on my death bed thinking, "I wish I had written my book."

The third reason I gave my writing coach was this affirmation: "I AM good enough." When I uttered those words, part of me was still processing whether those words were true! I couldn't believe I had actually given that as an answer! But there it was, from my own mouth: I AM GOOD ENOUGH! It was as if my mouth finally found the courage to affirm what my spirit already knew. But I also know that maintaining that freedom and truth does not come without a FIGHT!

This book is for those of you who don't feel like you are good enough! This book is for those of you who have long felt that you would never realize your dreams. This book is for those of you who have been told that you wouldn't amount to very much. This book is for those of you who have allowed yourself to believe that what other people thought of you had to become your reality (news flash, it doesn't!) This book is for those of you who, like Simone, have a secret dream, a goal, a vision, a desire, a passion; and yet you also have a reservation, a fear, a doubt, a pessimistic outlook. This book is for those of you who, like me, did not have a great start in life, weren't born on the "right" side of the tracks with a silver spoon in your mouth, and never felt good enough to do what others said was impossible. I give you permission today to stop lying to yourself! You have to do this! You are good enough! This book is for you! The journey starts with faith!

Questions to Ponder

1) What do you really want to do in your life?

2) What fears are keeping you from moving forward with your plan?

3) Who (or what) informed your belief that you aren't good enough to do anything you really want to do?

4) Are you willing to see yourself reaching your goals? How can you be so sure? Why now?

5) If you were on your deathbed today, what have you not done that you WISH you had done?

2
FAITH

"Faith is to believe what we do not see, and the reward for this faith is to see what we believe."
~Saint Augustine

That evening after speaking with Simone, I felt so ready to write this book, except for one tiny problem: I had never actually written a book! But I couldn't shake the feeling that this was the time; TODAY was the day! As I got in my car and drove out of the parking garage, I was motivated! Driving along the freeway at the end of rush hour, I felt free! I couldn't wait to get home and tell my wife that I was *finally* going to write my book! "Wait! I can't tell her that! She's going to think I'm joking since I've been telling her that for years," I convinced myself. And just like that, I was starting to talk myself right out of my destiny the same way Simone tried to do in my office. I sat there at the red light around the corner from my subdivision. Suddenly, I was fearful. I started to become discouraged. "Well, it was a fun thought while it lasted," I said to myself.

But just then, a bumper sticker in front of me captivated my attention. It said, "Let your faith be bigger than your fears!" In my life, I've come to believe that there is no such thing as coincidence. We are wherever we are exactly when we are supposed to be there. So immediately I started to try to find the "deeper meaning" behind why I was at that light at that exact moment reading that bumper sticker. Let your faith be bigger than your fears! Sometimes all it takes is a gentle reminder that you are not alone. For me, that bumper sticker was just the reminder I needed to confirm that my fear was a valid feeling and that faith is a remedy for overcoming fear.

No doubt, you've heard many definitions of faith. "Faith is the substance of things hoped for and the evidence of things not seen" (Hebrews 11:1). "Faith is taking the first step even when you don't see the whole staircase" (attributed to Dr. Martin Luther King, Jr.). Those are great definitions. My definition is this: ***"Faith is believing what you know is true even if you don't yet believe that what you know is true!"*** Over the years, I have discovered that faith means different things to different people. But four areas in my life have helped me cultivate an effective faith-based lifestyle: Faith in God, faith in myself, faith in my destiny, and faith in my failure.

Faith in God

One of my favorite daily affirmations is from the Unity Church. I say this to myself every morning and at least a few times throughout the day: "God is unlimited good, everywhere present. Therefore, God is within me. I seek and find the presence and power of God within me. I give thanks for this truth: Wherever I am, God is. I cannot go where God is not. I find God in me, in others, and in all my experiences, always. Whenever I begin anew, I am grateful for the new possibilities before me."

Whether one chooses to refer to God as God, "a Higher Power," "The Presence That Is," or "The Essence of All," my point is that having faith in God is the foundation for achieving anything you want in life. Since I believe that God created the earth and humankind, I believe God created us all to accomplish a purpose on this earth! You're probably thinking, "Wait, but you said your mother was a 19-year-old unwed, drug-addicted prostitute." YEP! So then how could God possibly be in that? Good question. Answer: the same way that God is in everything else. And God *still* created me to accomplish a purpose on this earth! Don't ever let anyone tell you that because of "how" you got here, you were a mistake! WRONG! You were never a mistake! God knew that you would be here because God alone created you! Yes, the "act" of making a child may have involved two people, but in the mind of God, you were never a mistake or an accident.

You were created because YOU have a specific purpose to accomplish on this earth in the time you have been allotted! That alone should be enough to encourage you that YOU ARE GOOD ENOUGH! God did not just create us to take up space in the universe. Since God created us for a purpose, on some level, I believe that God is "in all (our) experiences, always!" Therefore, my faith in God is foundational to faith in myself.

<u>Faith in yourself</u>

We're friends, right? So let me be transparent. This was the hardest area of the four that I had to conquer. It is easy to have faith in God because, well, I mean, God is God—who argues with that? But it was so difficult for me to envision a life where I could have faith in myself *until* I started to internalize the idea that *"God is within me. I seek and find the presence and power of God within me."* When we understand that we are intertwined with God, it helps us to know that WE ARE GOOD ENOUGH!

When I was little, I used to love to watch a cartoon called "Popeye the Sailor Man." In Popeye's own power, he was pretty weak. But whenever Popeye opened a can of spinach and ate it, suddenly he found superhuman strength to do whatever he needed to do! Now I must admit that I'm not a huge fan of spinach. But I am a huge fan of regularly "eating faith." How does one "eat faith," you ask? By speaking what you believe EVEN IF you don't yet believe it! The more I allowed people to speak for me and to tell me that I wasn't going to be this or that, the more those words found their way into my system!

When I decided to encourage myself and speak positive and optimistic thoughts, I noticed that what I was saying started to become true! It's not always easy to have faith in yourself, believe me, I get it! But think about it, if you're anything like me, you're GREAT at being the cheerleader for everyone else! People come to you for advice because they know you will encourage them and inspire them to do whatever they want to do! So if we can encourage other people to have faith in themselves...wait for it...what does it look like that we don't have faith in our own abilities? That's fear! Fear is the enemy of faith! Don't let fear win!

By the way, if it is true that God created us, then why would God create us to be scared of ourselves? It's as if we are afraid of our own shadow at times. But the shadow is only a reflection of who we really are...it is not another person! Even if you don't believe that you have faith in yourself, START TELLING YOURSELF that you DO! No, I'm serious! Right now...try it, "I have faith in myself!" Again, "I have faith in myself!" The more you affirm what you believe, the more it will start to manifest itself into your permanent psyche. After all, you are responsible for accomplishing the purpose for which you were created, your destiny!

Faith in your destiny

So, humor me this: When I was growing up, you name it, I wanted to be it! I wanted to be a fireman, a policeman, a lawyer, a doctor, and a football player, all at once. Of course, when you're nine years old sitting in Career Day at school, you start to believe you can be anything you want. Well, over time, I realized that I don't like heat so I sure won't like fire; I'm not a fan of guns; I always lose arguments; me and blood don't get along, and football, well, let's just say that the closest I ever came to a football field after my first time in football practice was being the waterboy, for one game...in my entire life. But from the time Mrs. Ballard "encouraged" (well, actually she "volun-told") me to recite a speech for a Black History Month presentation that earned me bragging rights in high school, I knew that my destiny would have something to do with speaking. When I graduated from high school, I was one of the graduation speakers. My topic was: "We Can! We Will! We Must Succeed!" (Oh, the irony of that speech and the premise of this book!) Even when I began preaching at the age of 19, I didn't fully understand that this was all part of the plan. This was all part of my destiny.

To date, I've spoken to hundreds of young people as a motivational speaker and thousands of people as a minister. Having faith in my destiny was not easy to come by because, well, to be honest, I never thought I was good enough to be "that guy" who used to be on the monitor in a church of 3,000 people in a small town in Central Georgia. But I'm learning to have faith that what I am called to do will create its own space, learning experiences, and triumphs for me. The same is true for you too. Maybe you're not called to be a public speaker, but whatever purpose you ARE created for will give you everything you need to be successful! Remember that definition of faith? ***"Faith*** *is believing what you know is true even if you don't yet believe that what you know is true!"* It applies to your destiny too!

In your heart, I believe you already know why you were created. (You might not want to share it with anyone because of your own fears, but yoooou know...admit it!) You have to believe that what you know is your destiny is truly for you even if you don't believe it right now. It has been more than 25 years since that day in Mrs. Ballard's class that started me toward the path of my destiny. When I look back at it now, I say to myself, "Wow! Whoever would have thought I would be here?!" Keep in mind that destiny is like a tree with branches that extend from the base. My destiny's base has been encouragement in public speaking, but everything else about which I have been passionate in life somehow relates back to that base, whether as a minister, a chaplain, a public speaker, and now, an author. Let me drop this on you. YOUR destiny is not about you! (Once more for the people in the balcony...) I said, "YOUR DESTINY IS NOT ABOUT YOU!" You were created on this earth to do something that will in one way or another benefit someone else! If your destiny is to be a chef, it's not so that you will be the only person to ever taste your delicacies—but it just might be so that you can become the main chef for an orphanage that serves over 400 children a day! Furthermore, you might end up creating a cookbook for children's recipes!

Maybe your destiny is to be a writer. It's not so that you can be the only person who reads your books! Perhaps the book you write will help someone decide against committing suicide! You might even end up becoming your own talk show host to help people work through life's difficulties! Just because your destiny is set doesn't mean it's set in stone. Be flexible! Be open! Be available! And most of all, be willing to fail and try again!

<u>Faith in your failure</u>

I will never forget the first time I gave a sermon. (In my church they call it a "trial sermon" for a reason.) It was horrible. My voice was cracking. My points didn't make sense, I lost my place in the Bible, I forgot to look at my audience to keep good eye contact. When I finished, I knew I had failed miserably because the people in the audience gave me "that look" as if to say, "Um, yeah. Well, you can always be a football pl—never mind. Just sit down." That was one of the most embarrassing ten minutes of my entire life. I didn't understand at the time that my failure in that moment would only serve to help me later in life.

I have discovered that failure has its place in your destiny. I can tell you that I do not like to fail. I like to win! I will play video games over and over again until I've conquered them because I refuse to lose. I'm "that guy" who always calls "do over" in Uno and other card games if somehow I find myself losing. But when it comes to your destiny, sometimes failure is the only way that you can GET where you really need to be!

It's not until you fail that you really gain an appreciation for what it's like to win. Failure helps you to find your footing! Failure keeps you humble because it's not until you fail that you really realize that you CAN fail and that you're not perfect. Failure helps you to understand that YOU ARE GOOD ENOUGH because failure gives you more than one opportunity to excel!

Having faith in your failure means you are open to the notion that everything happening now has a greater purpose later. Having faith in your failure means that even when things don't go well, you know there is always tomorrow; another chance to try again...another chance to do what you wanted—better! Failure is only part of the process. In other words, failure is not a destination; failure is a rest stop! Failure gives you time to regroup and start over again with new information that can help you perfect your original idea.

As a person who believes that "wherever I am, God is," I know that even when I fail, I am never alone. God is with me to help soothe the blow of the failure and help me get up and try again. Sometimes failure can also help you realize when you are not operating in your destiny.

For example, the first time I was on the field to try to learn how to play football, I knew that football was not in my destiny; everyone around me knew—hence the waterboy assignment, and I couldn't even get that right! That is very different than giving up on something that you know you were created to do. Failing at my first sermon was not the end of the road for me because I knew God had blessed me with a gift; part of the failure came from trying to mimic what I had seen other preachers do rather than embracing my own style and living my own truth.

When you have faith in your failure, your faith and your failure will guide you to what you did wrong and how you were not being authentically you. My grandmother used to say, "You can run from a lot of people, but you'll never be able to run from yourself. You can't hide from you!" So allow your failure to be your guide! After all, life is no fun if everything goes perfectly every time! When you have faith, it helps you to appreciate your dreams, visions, and the imagination with which you have been blessed!

There is an old gospel song with the lyrics, "Nobody told me that the road would be easy..." Cultivating an attitude of faith is not easy. It is a daily fight for me to *believe what I know is true even if I don't yet believe what I know is true.* But that's why I can appreciate the way that God, myself, my destiny, and my failure have all worked together to develop me into the person I am today. Fighting the good fight of life starts with faith! When you have faith, your imagination can soar! After all, God is within you!

Questions to Ponder

1) What is YOUR definition of faith?

2) What (or Who) do you consider to be your "Higher Power?" It's important to name this so that you can always refer back to this power when you get stuck.

3) Who told you that you shouldn't believe in yourself? How do you now know that they were wrong?

4) What is your destiny? What is the extension of your destiny?

5) What failure did you think was the end?

3
IMAGINATION

"Live out of your imagination, not your history..."
~Stephen Covey

A few weeks ago, I took my four-year-old Jada with me to run some errands. As we were riding along, I noticed that my daughter was talking with one of her toy dolls she was holding in her hand. They were engaged in quite the conversation about drawing in school and "making good choices." Eventually, I asked, "Who are you talking to?" When she told me that it was her doll, I asked, "How are you having a conversation with her if she can't talk back to you?" Of course, four-year-olds have an answer for everything. Without missing a beat, she responded, "She is talking back to me, Daddy. You just have to use your imagination to hear her!" That encounter inspired me to rethink everything I thought I knew about destiny, vision, and faith.

Many people believe imagination is just for children, but it's not. All of us have been gifted with an imagination. All of us have been gifted with creativity to achieve the destiny for which we have been created. Sometimes we get so caught up in the humdrum, mundane routines of life that we "choose" not to make time to explore our imagination. But it's there; it's always there! Think about it. How many times have you found yourself driving past the lottery sign and wondering what you would do if you won the $441-million-dollar jackpot? How many times have you watched a television show and started daydreaming about your favorite actor or actress? Perhaps you even started daydreaming about being an actor or an actress. That's your imagination at work!

The same thing is true for accomplishing your destiny. God has gifted you with an imagination in order to map out what your destiny should look like! Now, granted, not everyone is going to win the $441-million-dollar jackpot; it's just not going to happen for most people. But when you can use your mind's eye to visualize your passion, that's your imagination saying, "Hey, pay attention! You can do this! YOU ARE GOOD ENOUGH!"

Just a few decades ago, who would ever have dreamed of the kind of technology we have today? As I am writing this chapter, I'm having a face-to-face video conversation with my daughter on my phone. That was the result of someone's imagination. Our cars can talk to us and help us make decisions; our smart phones are often smarter than we are! In fact, every invention around us is the result of someone allowing themselves to believe in the power of their imagination.

Can you imagine what would have happened if the inventor of the cell phone had never spoken out about that invention? (I can. We would still be looking for change for pay phones, or worse yet, we would still be using rotary phones with the long telephone cord that could stretch throughout the entire house. Thank God for technology). Can you imagine what would have happened if the inventor of GPS had never spoken out about that invention? (I can. I would still have absolutely no sense of direction). In recognizing that YOU ARE GOOD ENOUGH, it's important to remember that your imagination is a huge part of the way God made you.

You can't achieve what you don't imagine!

Have you ever been watching television and saw a commercial and said to yourself, "Ah, that should have been my invention!" Well, yes, it probably could have, but since it wasn't, what else *have you been* imagining? I've already talked about my struggle with feeling inadequate to write a book. This has been years in the making. But it wasn't until one day I was sitting on my bed staring at the ceiling daydreaming about the cover of my book that it started to come together in my mind. Yes, there are going to be challenges to every imagination. Rarely does everything come as a thought and within minutes it is complete. But if you never allow yourself to imagine the impossible, how do you expect it to happen?

Simone, for example, was able to imagine herself as a nurse. That was half the battle for her! Once you can *see* it, you can *achieve* it! But many of us sell ourselves short because of our limited vision. Don't ever lose the gift of your imagination! When my daughter told me that I could hear her doll if I used my imagination, she then forced me to have a conversation with the doll. (Of course, if you know my daughter, you know that she also told me exactly what the doll was trying to tell me based on her imagination, but you get the point!)

Imagination is specific to you!

Just because someone else doesn't see what you can see about your future doesn't mean it is not a good idea or that it is not supposed to happen. Not everyone can see what you can see because it is not their imagination. As a matter of fact, everyone is not *supposed* to be able to see your imagination! For example, I recently heard on the radio that a certain bookseller was creating a device that would make it possible for their delivery drivers to open the door of your home and leave a package for you. (Of course, you have to purchase a security camera/smart lock bundle, but the concept is genius!) Now, can you imagine what that conversation must have been like when the inventor of the smart lock product brought it to the product vetting committee? I'm sure that inventor was met with a lot of resistance and people who believed that it would never work. However, apparently, this has become a pretty popular delivery method that will soon take off in numerous cities across the country.

What is for you is for you. Other people don't have to embrace your ideas, your vision, or your passion. If they were supposed to have it, they would have been gifted with it. Don't ever let someone tell you that what you've imagined is impossible. Maybe it's not for *them* to imagine. The idea was given to you. Look around you. Everything you see was once just an idea in someone's imagination—from the recliner in which you're comfortably reading this book, to the music that is playing on your iPod while you read—imagination is important! Remember, once you can see it, you can achieve it! Don't be afraid of what you see! Someone's life may depend on YOUR dream coming true!

Imagination is not coincidental!

Remember when I mentioned that no matter how you came about, you are not a mistake? Well, guess what, there is no such thing as coincidence when it comes to your imagination either. "God" is not sitting around somewhere saying, "Oh my, I can't believe (he or she) came up with that idea! I wonder where that came from!" No, it's no coincidence that you're imagining what you want to achieve or become in life. That was part of the plan all along! You were created for this time, this season, this purpose, this DESTINY! Yes, you! Don't pass up this wonderful opportunity to do what you *really* want to do! If you're that passionate about something, you must listen to your heart! There's a reason something is burning so deeply on the inside.

Often times with my patients and family members, I will say, "Do you realize that one left turn literally changed the entire course of your life?" The same is true for imagination. All it takes is one spark of creativity; one spark of passion; one spark of belief and believe me, you can make an entire fireworks display! I believe nothing happens to us by accident. Even our thoughts are not an accident! We have all been given a purpose! It's up to us to live out that purpose in the world!

The fight for many of us is allowing ourselves to dream and to imagine! We cannot allow ourselves to be afraid of what we see. Someone is waiting for our dream to come to pass! (Remember, our destiny is not about us; it's about others.) Someone is waiting for you to do what's in your heart—that dream that is keeping you awake at night imagining the greatness that can come from it...yes, someone is waiting for YOU to do it! The gift of our imagination is one of the greatest gifts that we have! Don't waste it! Once you have something in your mind, set some goals and make it happen! How many times are you going to watch that commercial and think, "That should have been me!" Well, guess what? NOW is the time for it TO be you! YOU ARE GOOD ENOUGH to make this happen! Go for it!

Imagination is dynamic!

When I first started college, I was under the impression that whatever major I chose, I was required to stick with that major for the duration of my program. I quickly learned that the first two years were primarily dedicated to general education classes and some core courses, which helped give me an idea of a wide range of academic options. This was helpful to me because I realized there were so many things I wanted to do in life, and there were so many potential programs that matched my general goal.

For example, early on I sensed that I wanted to major in psychology. But I wasn't sure if I wanted to major in organizational, general, industrial, or even forensic psychology. Having the opportunity to take some core psychology classes and electives, I was able to figure out pretty quickly that social psychology was a good fit because it used concepts from all the fields of psychology.

Imagination is the same way. Just because you imagine your life and goals in one way today doesn't mean you have to keep those same goals and dreams. In fact, drawing from that $441-million-dollar lottery win analogy, I can assure you that every time the lottery reaches such a high amount that I feel "compelled" to play, I have a different idea about how I would want to spend that money. At one point in my life, my dream winnings were all about me: I wanted a new house, a new car, and all the fried chicken that money could buy. As years went on, I started to become more interested in charitable giving. So I imagined that if I won the lottery, I would give to some of my favorite charities. My imagination changed and that was ok.

Maybe you used to have a particular dream and over time, you're not as sure that it complements where you are now in your life. That's ok! My point is that as your imagination changes, you should flow with your imagination. Don't get so set in your imaginative ways that you obstruct your creativity. It could be that your imagination is trying to show you how to improve upon your initial idea. But it could also be that your imagination is trying to draw out of you untapped ideas and potential that you didn't even see coming! Stay open in your imaginative process.

Since that conversation with my daughter about her dolls talking back to her, I've learned that all her dolls have families of their own. They now all attend school and are looking forward to having siblings. (This was not the plan in the initial conversation). But my daughter continues to imagine each day with her dolls; she creates their reality for them and it is prone to change at any time. May we be open to whatever our imagination imagines!

Questions to Ponder

1) When you were small, what kinds of things did you imagine you would be (or create)?

2) As you look over your life, what kinds of things make you smile when you daydream about them today?

3) Who are some of the people that have told you that your ideas would never work? How do you now know that they are wrong?

4) What have you already imagined (and seen come to pass) in your life that at one point you thought was impossible?

4

GOALS

"People with goals succeed because they know where they're going!"
~Earl Nightingale

I am old enough to remember the days when we had to purchase and use a road map to get from one place to another. Sometimes it took forever to figure out how you were going to get from Point A to Point B. (Is that a lake we have to cross? How does this road intersect with that road? Why are there fifteen hundred names for one stretch of road anyway?) These days, we have this wonderfully remarkable invention known as a global positioning system, or GPS. Just by entering data into a small device, you can have directions for traveling just about anywhere within a matter of seconds. As a person who values time and likes to get where I'm going as quickly as possible, the GPS saves me a lot of time and headache.

A few weeks ago, I got in my car with every intention of driving from Georgia to South Carolina along a very familiar route. I've driven the same route hundreds of times to South Carolina, so I didn't feel the need to use the GPS. After all, I knew where I was going. But there were two problems: first, the location I thought was my final destination had moved. I wasn't aware that the building had moved to an entirely different town in South Carolina. Second, on the way, traffic was backed up because of a major accident on the road ahead of me. So instead of using my handy GPS to help me navigate around the accident, I just assumed I could figure it out on my own.

I got off the freeway and started taking back roads, through Georgia, at night. Bad idea! There were very few street lights. There were very few businesses along the route, and the lone gas station I encountered did not seem like a very safe and friendly place to stop and ask for directions. Then, to make matters worse, because I was in the middle of nowhere when I finally tried to engage the GPS for assistance, I saw those dreaded words flash across the screen: "Searching for Network." That made for a very long ride. Ironically, after driving around on back roads for an hour, I realized that if I had the assistance of the GPS, I could have been well on my way within about five minutes of taking the right turns. I learned some valuable lessons that day about GPS and about life.

Part of my life's challenge in feeling I was not good enough to realize my dreams is that I often did not have a clear plan for how I wanted to achieve them. It's one thing to have a great vision along with a great imagination. But if you don't have a plan to execute the vision, you will continue to spin your wheels. This was my problem. Many times, we trick ourselves into believing that we are not good enough because we have this great vision, but no plan to carry it out. Or worse yet, rather than laying out a plan, we figure, "Oh, that will be easy. I know what I'm doing" only to discover that when something happens to throw us off our path, we have no clue how to successfully recover.

As a result, we waste countless hours, days, and years trying to get back on track when we might have been able to quickly recover if only we had a plan. YOU ARE GOOD ENOUGH to do whatever you want to do. YOU ARE GOOD ENOUGH to accomplish all of the dreams for which God created you. But it helps to have a well-thought-out plan to help you achieve your goals.

Enter your destination

The first step in using the GPS (and in setting your goals) is to have an idea of where you want to go! Someone once said that if you don't know where you're going, any road will get you there. Well, anyone who has used a GPS, for example, knows that the destination can sometimes be misleading. For example, the other day I was in an unfamiliar town in Georgia and I wanted to find a McDonald's. I entered McDonald's into the GPS and suddenly every McDonald's within a 200-mile radius showed up on my screen. That was not helpful for me, because I only wanted one restaurant in one small town. In order to set your goal, you have to have a clearly defined destination.

Where do I really want to go? Is my goal short-term or long-term? (Hint: if you have no idea, it's usually best to start with a short-term goal.) I have found that it is easier for me to function when I have clearly defined short, intermediate, and long-term goals. Why? I'm glad you asked. I never want to feel like I have nothing else to look forward to. Part of being GOOD ENOUGH (for me) is knowing that I have something to contribute to the world on an ongoing basis.

Once I was able to accept that I DO matter to the world, to God, and to myself, I started this perpetual journey toward continual contribution. In other words, I always have a goal for a project or initiative that I'm working on that will contribute to the well-being of myself and others. Whenever I start to feel like I have nothing more to contribute, I run the risk or falling back into the bowels of depression; I don't ever want to feel that way again. But when I start a project, I always start by figuring out where I want to be when I get where I'm going!

Let's take writing this book, for example. My destination was: I'm going to write a book called FIGHT: From Not Enough to Good Enough. When I first started writing, that was all I had, a title. I didn't know how the chapters were going to be formed. I didn't know (at the time) that FIGHT was an acronym for fight, imagination, goals, help, and time. All I had was an idea and an end goal.

My short-term goal was to hire a book/writing coach and to develop an outline. Check! My long-term goal was to have a professional cover designed and to have the book self-published. Check! But all the while, I knew that my destination was going to be the book that you hold in your hand. Just like with the GPS, when I first did a search for the title of my book (to make sure it had not already been taken), sure enough, I found all kinds of similar titles, but none that were exactly like mine. That was confirmation enough that I was starting off toward the right destination.

You must be clear about what YOU want for YOUR life. Stop living someone else's expectations or dreams for you. The only person who truly matters is God and YOU, and since "wherever you are, God is" that should be much simpler. Part of feeling that I was not enough came from the fact that I was never able to please the people I thought I needed to please, my adoptive parents.

If I knew then what I know now, I would have spent far less time worrying about trying to please them, and far more time carving out my own destiny based on what God wanted for my life. As a result, here I am in my early 40s finally writing a book I've dreamed about since I was in my 20s—all because I felt like writing a book wasn't enough for me to be considered good enough. Can you imagine what my life would have been like if I had come to this realization twenty years ago? I would likely be much further along. Don't be like I was! Wherever you are, it's never too late to imagine the best life you can have! It's never too late to start figuring out exactly where you are trying to go and deciding the best route to get there!

One more thing: you have to start somewhere, so start where you are! Sometimes we get so caught up in trying to duplicate what we think someone else's process has been that we sabotage our own success. But each of us has a process to follow. Each of us has a "lane" we've been assigned to. It's up to us to start where we are in order to get where we are going. Don't worry about trying to do too much at once. Start where you are! If all you have is the title of your first book, great! That's a start! If you all you have right now is an idea for a business that you want to start, great! Work with what you have until you have what you've worked!

Watch out for distractions

My GPS is really good about keeping me informed of potential hazards or distractions. (Watch out: vehicle stopped on shoulder ahead! Watch out: hazard on road ahead! Watch out: police reported ahead! And my favorite: Watch out: traffic reported ahead; and during Atlanta rush hour, estimated time in traffic: four hours and fifteen minutes). The GPS is a lifesaver when it comes to helping me navigate around distractions. Setting effective goals can do the same for you! Whenever you are trying to do something to better yourself or for the benefit of others, there will always be distractions (not enough money or resources, not enough support, not enough of this or that). But in reality, distractions are just part of the process. But having clear and measurable goals helps you work around life's distractions.

As I was writing this book, I set a goal of writing one chapter per week. Of course, if I was spending six or seven weeks in the mountains with few distractions, that would have been an easily achievable goal. But I have a family, a career, civic duties, a personal life, and I pastor a church. It seemed like whenever I wanted to write, I was "just too tired." Well, guess what I realized? That was an excuse! People make time for who and what they deem most important! MY truth was that when I first started writing this book, years ago, I was still enveloped in all the fears I mentioned earlier, so I allowed my distractions to take me away from accomplishing my goals.

Many of you can relate to making excuses to get out of doing what you really know in your heart you're destined to do. If you're anything like me, you're great at making excuses; some of my favorites: "I'm too busy. I'm too tired. I don't have the right resources. I don't even know where to start. My daughter needs me. I have to work overtime. My honey-do list is getting longer and longer (knowing good and well I've still not started on that list)." Excuses are nothing more than distractions designed to keep you from reaching your goal. STOP IT! I know, I know. You're saying, "But it's not that simple!" Actually, yes, it is that simple! If you really want something, you have to work for it and stop at NOTHING to make it happen! Stop using excuses. They are only keeping you from getting where you want to be!

It wasn't until I recognized my worth and what I have to offer that I was able to set and keep this goal. In fact, when I became really committed to this task, I found that I was reaching my goals earlier and earlier because I didn't allow my distractions to get in the way. Rather than taking weeks to write one chapter, I was able to use a couple days to write a chapter, which freed up a couple more days to make edits. Knowing that you have a goal in mind helps you to stay focused on your goal and free from distractions. Intentionality is key! Intentionality requires discipline. You can do it, but it's up to you to work your plan and stick to your goal!

Recalculating

You're moving along toward your destination and suddenly you hear, "recalculating." That usually means one of two things. Either you've missed a turn along the way and you need to get refocused or you're about to encounter some sort of hazard up ahead that requires using a different route. It used to frustrate me when my GPS would recalculate my route, until I started to understand my GPS settings. My GPS is designed to get me from Point A to Point B using the fastest route possible with the least amount of traffic. Sometimes what I think is the best route might not actually be the best route. I've learned to (in general) trust that the GPS knows something I don't know and follow the route that has been recalculated for me.

In life, you're going to have to recalculate many times based on your goals. Sometimes where you thought you were going ends up being a very different direction. You might end up meeting the love your life and getting married, recalculating. You might end up getting pregnant, recalculating. You might end up with an unexpected promotion on your job, recalculating. Conversely, someone very close to you might die, recalculating. You might lose the job from which you thought you were going to retire, recalculating. You might end up losing everything you owned and find yourself homeless, recalculating. Life has a way of throwing some very good and bad curve balls. But that doesn't have to change your goal.

Just because life may come at you hard and fast doesn't mean that you have to forfeit your dream or your goal. It might take you longer to get where you want to be, but trust that if it's your goal and your desire, you will reach it. Don't ever let someone tell you that because of what you've done or because of what you've experienced you can't reach your goal. Yes, you might have to take a detour, but a detour is designed to get you around something that could hurt you. Detours are your friend, not your enemy!

Sometimes our life's GPS will recalculate a new route for us to make sure we don't try to take on too much at once. Even in setting goals, they must be realistic and achievable.

I like cake—a lot…especially chocolate cake. But trying to eat an entire chocolate cake at once will make me sick and tired (speaking from personal experience; don't try this at home folks.) I'm glad that you're starting to recognize your worth and the fact that YOU ARE GOOD ENOUGH! But that doesn't mean you have to try to conquer the world and everything you've ever wanted to do at one time. You'll burn yourself out and make yourself sick. When that happens, you're no good to anyone. For me, once I had that pivotal moment of realization, I decided to start by writing this book. From here, I'll start working on my next project, and then the next, until I have really started working down my ever-growing list of things I want to accomplish. You can do the same. Take your time. You'll get there!

You have arrived at your destination

I love to travel, but I especially love hearing my GPS say, "You have arrived at your destination." I started on a journey; I navigated all of the distractions. I took the required detours and followed the recalculated recommendations. Now I've finally arrived. I've reached my goal! So, here's the thing. Just because I've reached the goal doesn't mean that I roll down my window and throw out the GPS! No! The GPS is there for multiple trips and I will need it again. Yes, I set some goals for this dream or project, but there will be many others! I can attest to the fact that when you accomplish one dream, you want to start working on the next. Sometimes the rush of accomplishing one goal is all it takes to get you working on the next goal.

Having lived through the experience with my adoptive father and his wife, I knew what it was like to have someone tell me that I was not going to amount to much and that I likely wouldn't graduate from high school. Well, sometimes negative encouragement is all the positive energy you need! The more they told me what I wasn't going to be able to do, the more I was determined to make it happen. It wasn't easy. I wasn't a straight-A student. I needed tutors, special assistance, and a wing and a prayer a lot of times. But I graduated from high school!

When I joined the military, it took years of counseling and therapy for me to work through the negative effects of being told that I was not enough for so many years! But at the prompting of some of my friends, I decided to start another college degree. (The first few times I started college didn't go so well; I wasn't motivated and I didn't have the inner fortitude to believe that I was good enough for a degree!) But when I joined the Air Force, all of that changed. The military helped push me toward goals that I didn't even think were possible for myself.

One such goal was completing Korean studies at the Defense Language Institute Foreign Language Center. Who would ever have thought that someone who barely graduated high school would be able to learn and excel in a second language? But it happened! I earned an Associate degree in Korean and that propelled me forward to earn three more college degrees, including another Associate degree, a Bachelor's degree, and a Master's degree! If I can do it by setting goals and fighting for what I wanted for myself, believe me, YOU CAN TOO! The only person standing in your way is YOU! Move over and make room for yourself! I'm not saying it will be easy, and I'm certainly not saying you can do it on your own! All of us need help to get where we're going! But you CAN and WILL get there with the right goals!

Questions to Ponder

1) What are your top three goals for the next year?

2) If you could only choose one, which would it be and why?

3) What is your plan for reaching that goal? Short-term? Long-term? Intermediate?

4) What are some potential distractions that have kept you from realizing your dreams and how do you now know that you can overcome them?

5) What are some of the excuses that have kept you from moving forward?

5

HELP

"There is no need to suffer silently, and there is no shame in seeking help."
~Joel S. Manuel

Growing up feeling as though I was not good enough often made me feel I had to "prove" myself to everyone I met. I lived in a state of perpetual defensiveness because I felt I always had to fight to prove my worth or value. What I didn't realize at the time was that the only person I really had to convince was myself!

Whether other people believe I am good enough or not is their issue, not mine! I AM GOOD ENOUGH (and so are you!) If you believe that YOU ARE GOOD ENOUGH, then you ARE! You didn't get the job? Okay. It doesn't mean that you weren't good enough for the position; it simply means that "they" opted to go in another direction. (Hint: start your own business and work for yourself! Cut out the middle-person! That's all the confirmation you need!) The person you thought you were "destined" to be with chose someone else? Okay. It doesn't mean that you were not good enough. Have you considered that perhaps that person didn't feel they were good enough for you? Life is all about perspective.

In order for me to come to accept my own worth, I needed a lot of help! Don't think that because you're reading this book, one day I just woke up and had great self-esteem and all was well in my world! It wasn't. I can't even try to pretend that I am where I am in life because of my own strength. I needed the help of God, therapists, psychiatrists, friends, family, mentors, pastors, and I also needed to learn how to help myself!

Of all the tools I offer in this book, this one was probably the most difficult for me. It is the one with which I continue to struggle. Why? Because when I was younger, I was often made to feel as though I had to have all the answers—me, alone, by myself. If I didn't have all the answers, then there must have been something wrong with me. (I wasn't good enough, right? Wrong. But you get my point.) As I got older, that belief grew stronger, so much so that I wouldn't ask for help even when I knew I needed it!

But I've learned now that asking for help is not a weakness. In fact, it is a strength (and potentially a lifesaver). I had to retrain my mind to believe that getting help is both necessary AND acceptable. The sooner you learn how to ask for help, the sooner you will be able to overcome your challenges. The sooner you overcome your challenges, the closer you will be to recognizing your value AND accomplishing your goals, objectives, and dreams. But as with everything else in life, learning to ask for help is a process!

The pride complex

Part of my goal in this book is to be transparent because I believe that we can learn from each other. If someone can learn from my hard times, maybe they can avoid having a similar situation. As much as I don't like to admit this, here it is: I like to feel like I'm in control, like I'm in charge, like I know what I'm doing and what's going on. I don't like to feel ill-equipped to perform any task or to achieve any goal. Anything less than perfection has often made me feel like I was less of a man.

Pride is one of the major challenges that had kept me in this self-induced cycle of shame and unworthiness. You see, it's not that there weren't people who were willing to gladly assist me; it's that I was too prideful to ask for the help I needed. I didn't want people to know that I wasn't perfect, that I had flaws, and that I was struggling.

One example of this occurred right after graduating from seminary. I had already secured a position as a chaplain resident with a prominent Atlanta area hospital. But there was a three-month gap between graduation and the time I was to start the paid residency. That summer, I worked a few odds-and-ends jobs to make the bare ends meet, but it was not enough to pay the bills long term. By the beginning of the residency year, there was another gap of about a month before we received our first paycheck. During this time, I was no longer working the part-time jobs, and no income was coming in. As a result, I had to move out of the rooming house in which I was living.

I was essentially homeless, so I slept in my car; no, I lived in my car in the parking lot directly across from the hospital. In the morning, I would wake up around 5 a.m., go into the hospital to wash up, shave, and iron a shirt in my office before anyone else arrived. I worked my full shift as a chaplain resident, and then I hung around until people started asking questions about why I was staying so late. I then returned to my car and started over the next day. When I needed to wash clothes, I made up some excuse (translation: lie) to one of my friends or church members about why I couldn't go to the laundromat. For food, I ate when I could, but as God and luck would have it, hospital employees love to have gatherings with food. There was always an abundance of food and leftovers.

During one of our interpersonal relationship groups, one of my fellow chaplain residents made a comment about how much of a struggle the residency process had been. In that moment, I snapped. "You want to know about struggle? Let me tell you about struggle!" I then went on to recount how the first few weeks of the program were really going for me.

When I had finished, my group and my supervisor looked at me in disbelief. Not only were they sad that I had been through so much, some of them expressed their frustration and anger with me for not asking them for help. I convinced myself that no one would understand my pain. My pride was a barrier to my progress. Here I was, the oldest person in a group of chaplains, but I didn't have a place to live. I was in one of the premier educational programs for chaplains in the world! In my mind, I worried that if the system found out I was homeless, they would no longer want me as part of their program. I had created all kinds of narratives in my head about what my group thought about me and my "struggle." Surely they would think that I wasn't "good enough" to be in their program. But to my surprise, my group was very understanding. Who knew that other people had struggles that were just as devastating as mine? We cried together, we prayed together, and then with the assistance of my group and supervisor, we devised a plan that helped me obtain stable housing until our pay started.

That was a tremendous turning point in my life. It helped me learn that I am just as human and susceptible to "life happening" as the people I spend my entire life helping. If people allow themselves to be vulnerable enough to come to me for help, who am I to allow my pride to keep me from asking for help? Here's my point: your pride is not worth your progress. The sooner we check our pride at the door, the sooner we can start to live up to our worth.

Don't be afraid to ask for help. What's the worst that can happen? (If you're anything like me, you can come up with a thousand different possibilities for what "could" happen, when in reality, the worst that could happen is that someone says they cannot help or support us.) But when we allow ourselves to be vulnerable enough to ask for help, somehow or another, help always has a way of finding us!

"I got it! Or so I thought!"

Sometimes our unwillingness to ask for help isn't necessarily related to pride. Sometimes it comes from a genuine desire to demonstrate our competence or confidence in our ability to thrive and succeed. But sometimes it also comes from our shame. What do I mean? Sometimes we feel like we "should have overcome this obstacle already," so it feels shameful when we realize that we are faced with the same demon.

It's bad enough to have others telling us that we shouldn't believe in ourselves, but what happens when we feel like "maybe they're right?" There are times when we feel like we shouldn't "have to" ask for help because we "shouldn't be going through this again." But guess what? Life is life. Just because you won one battle doesn't mean that you will win them all. But when we do get to that place where we feel like we've failed, we have to be willing to help ourselves!! In other words, we can't always believe that we're capable of doing everything or being "all things to all people." In order to really adopt the mantra that YOU ARE GOOD ENOUGH, you must be willing to get the help that you need.

As one might imagine from knowing my upbringing, I struggled with major depression for many years well into adulthood. At one point, I wanted to commit suicide so often that it was suspicious to me when I actually had what might be considered a "good day." My entire life felt like it was just one dark day after another. I had to force myself to get out of bed some days. Other days I just stayed in bed and didn't care one way or another if I lost my job, my home, my family, or anything else. I was a professional "happy" person. I knew how to play the role of the person who was always happy, always smiling, always seemed to be content with life. But inside, I was dying. I felt the weight of the world on my shoulders all the time, and guess what, the world is heavy!

Little did I know at the time, I was carrying the weight of my past on my shoulders. I was carrying the weight of all the unmet expectations of others on my shoulders. I was carrying on my shoulders the weight of adoptive parents who had their own issues and chose to take them out on me. I was carrying all this weight and had no idea what to do with it or how to "make do" with it.

I had been through therapy when I was in the military and when I was discharged. Therapy was ok, but it seemed like all those therapists wanted to re-open the wounds of my past and rehash them repeatedly in every session. That's one approach, but I found that it wasn't helpful for me. In fact, that approach helped me hide behind my pain, and in some ways, I was able to use that pain as a manipulation tool to get people to feel sorry for me. (When you feel like you're not good enough, it's easy to play the victim and have people eating out of your hand. But when you are free, you realize that you no longer have to play the victim because you don't need or desire anyone's sympathy. YOU ARE GOOD ENOUGH in your own right!)

During one depressive episode, I reached out to a therapist in my local area named Kerry. During our first session, I realized that she was going to challenge me in a way that felt, at once, both uncomfortable and liberating. As I started my "typical therapy story" of my past and how this happened to me and that happened to me, it was as if I could see and hear the "woe is me" song playing in her mind.

Kerry patiently let me finish my story and then, as gently but as directly as she could, she said something to the effect of, "Well, I hate to hear all that happened to you. But if you choose to live your life from that perspective, you'll never be able to appreciate where you are in life now!" That was hard for me to hear! I spent most of my adult life living from the perspective of a man broken from the time my mother abandoned me as an infant. Believe it or not, that narrative was a safe cocoon for me because, again, I could be the victim and get all the sympathy I wanted. When I was challenged to live in the now and to create the life I wanted to see for myself by capitalizing on my strengths rather than my vulnerabilities, life took on a whole new meaning.

When I first shared with Kerry that I wanted to write a book, she said, "So write a book!" To which I would respond, "Well what if nobody reads it?" Her immediate response was, "So what?! If you want to write a book, do it for YOU! Stop worrying about what other people will or won't do. If YOU believe in your book, other people will believe in your book." Then we moved on to discussing something else. I'm laughing as I write this paragraph because as much as it took me a while to get used to her direct, "no chaser" approach, her help propelled me to sit down and start writing, rather than just dreaming about it.

What I'm saying to you is, YOU CANNOT DO LIFE ALONE! Get some help! Like me, you did not wake up overnight feeling worthless or "less than" or incompetent. That took time to get into your soul and psyche. In the same way, it is going to take time to get that out of your soul and psyche. Sometimes the best way for this to happen is with the benefit of counseling/therapy. My hope for you is that you, too, will find a therapist like Kerry who can help you live the life you have now. There is no coincidence that we survived all those sleepless nights of depression, all those suicidal thoughts, all those times we wanted to give up. It was not for us to die. Someone is waiting on us to fulfill the destiny for which we were created!

Blocked blessings

I graduated from high school in 1993. My adoptive father and stepmother took me to the campus of Howard University in Washington, DC on August 15 of that year, dropped me off, and left me to fend for myself. Like many college students, expenses were high and funds were low. But I was blessed to secure a job as an assistant manager of the Blockbuster Video near campus. I wasn't broke or homeless, but there were times when I felt like I needed to rob Peter to pay Paul. I didn't have the support of my family at that time; I had essentially burned the bridge with my adoptive mother until years later. My adoptive father dropped me off and said, "Call me when you can't make it on your own anymore." I wasn't about to give him the satisfaction of ever believing that I was struggling or failing in life anymore.

During that first year of school, I started attending a church called Carolina Missionary Baptist Church. It was there that I first found my "voice" and felt a sense of call to ministry. Pastor Anthony Moore was the senior pastor of the church, and he was very supportive during my years there. He would do so much for me and never asked for anything in return. Additionally, many of the senior women in the church were the same way. Later, when I moved to Lynchburg, VA, I had a pastor named Pastor James Coleman and one of the church mothers from Court Street Baptist Church named Sis. Doris Reid who really took me under their wing and helped nurture and develop me. From these wonderful people and countless more, I learned a huge lesson about not blocking blessings.

You see, they all helped and supported me from the kindness of their heart. They never once asked for anything in return, except maybe that one day I pay the kindness forward. Because of my pride or my shyness (or whatever other excuse I could find), I often wanted to turn down their acts of generosity: money, food, lodging, clothes. But they all persisted, not in a forceful way, but in a way that helped me to know that I was loved and appreciated. But what is interesting about all of these people is they would all tell me that if I didn't accept their generosity, I was in effect blocking their blessings.

They said they weren't giving to me because of me, as much as they were giving to me because they felt compelled by God to give to me. They made comments like, "Well, you don't have to accept this money from me; think of it as coming from God." Or they said, "God told me to give this to you." Over time, that helped me understand that since God is within us, when people are kind enough to give, it is from their desire to be helpful. Let's face it, was there ever a time when someone gave you a generous blessing and you said, "Oh no, I couldn't possibly use this at all"?

If you're anything like me, the answer is no! But that hesitancy came from this fear that if they were offering me something, it must mean that they thought I was incapable of doing for myself, and therefore not good enough. Guess what? WRONG! In many cases, they were thinking "of" me, but they weren't thinking that at all "about" me. They did what they did because they knew their blessing was directly connected to their willingness to help me. Now I have learned to accept their blessings with genuine and gracious thanksgiving!

When people offer to help you, let them! Don't be so stuck on doing things "your way" that you cause someone else to miss out on perhaps one of their greatest blessings. You know that warm feeling you get inside when you're able to help someone else? Well, people get that warm feeling when they help us too! Recognizing that YOU ARE GOOD ENOUGH is not easy to do alone. Embrace the help that comes from God through others!

Questions to Ponder

1) In what areas of your life have you refused necessary help because of pride?

2) When did you realize you were at your breaking point and really needed help?

3) Is the help that you are currently receiving really helpful or do you need to make a change?

4) What can you do to help yourself make one self-improvement TODAY?

5) When was the last time you "blocked a blessing"? How might you have handled that differently after reading this chapter?

6
TIME

"Have patience with all things, but first of all, with yourself."
~Saint Francis de Sales

I've noticed that the older I get, the less time I want to waste on tasks that seem menial. For example, I don't like to grocery shop because the process takes too long. If I go into the store for sugar, I have to find the condiments aisle and then sift through 14 different brands and types of sugar to get what I want. I hate shopping for clothes just as much.

The other day I went into a department store to buy a white shirt. That's all, a simple white shirt. I walked into the store expecting that the sales clerk would understand the simplicity of my request and quickly direct me to a simple white shirt. Her response was, "What kind of simple white shirt?" She then proceeded to take me to the expansive shirt section; it was like white shirt paradise: long sleeve, short sleeve, V-neck, crew neck, shirts with buttons, shirts with no buttons, name brand shirts, knock-off shirts, off white, bright white, you get the point.

By the time we were done exploring all the white shirts, I didn't even want to buy a shirt anymore! What I thought would take just a few seconds ended up taking almost a half hour. I like getting things done, now!

Part of the reason I am such a stickler for time is that I feel so much of my life has been wasted by living my life through a negative lens. So I have often felt the need to try to enjoy as much of my "new" life as "good enough" in as productive and efficient manner as possible. I want to see everything, explore everything, and be everywhere at the same time.

On the other hand, I also have felt like getting to a place of being "good enough" should not take as long as it took me to accept and acknowledge. As much as I try to remind myself that life is a process and a journey, I often forget that every day I am not going to feel like I am on top of the world. Even now, I have days when I wake up temporarily feeling low or doubting whether I am really as valuable as I believe I am. That's a normal response for a person who has battled with years of feeling "less than" or "not enough."

Moving from not enough to good enough is a process that will take far more time than the time it took just to read this book. It will take time for you to accept, and it will take time for others to accept. In the meantime, there are a few things that you can do to help have a more successful and fruitful journey.

<u>Patience</u>

Shopping not included, I like to believe that I am one of the most patient people in the world—that is, when it comes to other people. But when it comes to myself, I am often one of the most impatient people I know. I'm sure this is related to setting standards for myself that may be unreasonably high. But one of the first keys to recognizing that YOU ARE GOOD ENOUGH is to be patient with the you that you were as well as the you that you want to become. Remember when I told you about my initial sermon?

Well, 22 years later, I'm still preaching sermons, but I like to think that in that time, I've become much more confident and much better at my delivery and oratorical presence. But it took time; it took failing miserably at times; it took starting over. But most of all, I knew that if I really wanted to survive as a minister or motivational speaker for the long term, it was going to take being patient with myself. I call this giving myself some grace. It's ok that I'm not always at the "top of my game." It's ok to have normal, temporary fears, but being patient with myself doesn't mean that I'm going backwards. It means that I'm recognizing and owning the fact that I'm not going to be perfect overnight or in the blink of an eye.

The same is true for you. Yes, you've been through a lot in life! But you are where you are, and it will take time to get where you want to be. Someone once told me that "anything worth having is worth waiting for." I believe that this is just as true for something like waiting for the "perfect mate" or giving yourself time to live your truth as a good enough creation of the Divine. Don't be so hard on yourself and expect that just because you "want" something different it will happen overnight. It won't.

You must remember that your life is as much a process as the next person's life. Be careful about comparing your life to someone else's. You never know what that person had to endure in order to become the person you see. Many people have the same struggles you have, but they've learned how to "fake it until (they) make it." I'm not advocating living a fake life; what I'm saying is that while you're assessing what appears to be someone else's "success," recognize that there are often struggles going on in the background about which no one knows. Be patient with yourself and patient with other people.

Stop and smell the roses

The other day my daughter and I were walking through the park on the way to the playground. As always, I was rushing to get her to the playground so she could wear herself out and get tired and get to her nap so that daddy could get some work done. My daughter moves at a snail's pace in general. It takes her forever to get dressed, put on her shoes, and walk to the car. But part of my daughter's reason for taking so long to do everything is that she is naturally curious.

As we were walking to the playground, her attention was drawn to a rose bush with some beautifully bloomed roses on them. My daughter stopped to look at the roses; she wanted to smell them. She wanted to tell me how pretty they were. She wanted to talk about how some roses were open and some were closed. As much as I wanted to get frustrated with her curiosity, I realized that she was teaching me a very valuable lesson; don't miss out on the beauty of the roses for trying to get to the playground. In that moment, she could have cared less about the swings, the sliding board, or the monkey bars. In that moment, she was only focused on the roses.

Many times in life, we are so busy trying to get to some goal in the future that we forget to embrace the beauty in the moment. Yes, I know this book is about getting from "not enough" to "good enough." But the reality is that even in those times when I've felt I was not enough, there were still some beautiful moments. The last two years of my high school life were emotionally stressful and discouraging, but I graduated!

Yes, I've attempted suicide a few times during the darkest nights of depression, but I survived…and I had assistance in getting back to a place of emotional stability. Yes, I was abandoned by my biological mother who was addicted to drugs and a prostitute, but I was later united with my biological brothers and sisters, with whom I continue to have a good and positive relationship to this day. Now whenever I see roses, I am reminded to pause and reflect on what is beautiful about the moment before me. In the same way, while you are moving toward becoming the person you want to be, ask yourself this: what is beautiful about you and your life right now?

The butterfly effect

I guess I must have been in second or third grade when I first learned about metamorphosis; the process through which a caterpillar becomes a butterfly. But the process itself is a good representation of the process one must endure in order to grow from feeling like not enough to owning that YOU ARE GOOD ENOUGH!

In the first stage, the eggs are laid on a plant that will provide food for the caterpillar. All of us had to come from somewhere. The environment in which we were born plays a tremendous part in the success or failure of our formative years. We don't get to decide where we come from, but here we are!

In the second stage, the caterpillar starts to grow inside the egg until it is large enough to break free. When this happens, the caterpillar eats the shell and the leaves of the plant on which the egg was laid. As we develop, we start to take into ourselves that which has been presented around us. Like me, many of us had to eat shells of defeat, discouragement, disappointment, disgust, and ridicule. We ate the leaves of the poisonous thinking, negative pronouncements over our lives, and painful abuses at the hands of the people who said they loved us.

In the third stage, the caterpillar produces a liquid from the glands below its mouth which hardens into a thread. The caterpillar attaches the thread to a twig or a leaf and spins a shell around its body. But while inside the shell, the caterpillar changes into the body of a butterfly. For many of us, the negative effects of our past have created a hard, emotional shell. Our shell grows larger and stronger because we try to find ways to burrow deeper and deeper into that place where we feel we can be safe from harm.

Here's where it gets tricky. This stage can take a few days or a few months. Many caterpillars don't survive this stage because they stop growing or they continue developing such a hard shell that, essentially, they are not able to break through and they end up dying in their shell. They've become a butterfly but they've not been able to break out of the shell so that they can get much-needed air to help them survive. In effect, they end up dying in their shell. I must admit, this was almost me. I was good at "smiling for the cameras" and making everybody think I was poised, confident, and had it going on. But inside, I was dying, because I didn't want people to see the real me—the one hidden deep within my shell.

Thankfully one day, I found the right support system; the right people to help me want more for myself. I found the strength to break free because, well, to be honest, I just got sick and tired of not being enough. I was determined to get to another level in my life. After all, if I had to be here, I was determined to make the best of it!

The final stage involves the butterfly inside the cocoon. The butterfly spreads its wings and the sheer strength of spreading the wings is enough to crack the shell. From there, the butterfly starts to pump air into its body, and when the blood starts to circulate, the butterfly is able to fly away! What an image! It's not always easy to spread our wings when we feel like we've been trapped inside a shell, suffocating for so long! But it's always worth trying and never giving up!

The more you grow, the more you spread. The more you spread, the more you'll be able to crack the shell that has been keeping you bound for so long. It's not until the butterfly comes out of the shell that it is able to get life-sustaining air that will help it to thrive. The same is true for us. Until we allow ourselves to really break free, we won't be able to receive the energy and vibes necessary for our survival. We get that energy from God, ourselves, and our support system. It's vitally important for us to know that good support often equates to good living. With the right support and by allowing the right energy into our spirit and psyche, we can reach the pinnacle of our dreams, goals, and desires.

Time to soar

Earlier I wrote about how my adoptive father said upon dropping me off at Howard University, "Call me when you can't make it on your own anymore." That was in 1993; he's still waiting on that call. Sometimes life forces you to soar. Sometimes you have no choice but to prove yourself and everybody else wrong. Sometimes the benefits of becoming better are much better than the reality of staying stuck in a revolving cycle of shame, hopelessness, and low self-esteem. But at some point, if you're anything like me, you just get to a place where you are sick and tired of being sick and tired! When I reached that point, rather than give up and die, I decided to make a change. It was not easy; change is never easy! But it is possible!

The first time I flew on an airplane, I was petrified. I didn't know what to expect. I was anxious, nervous, and uneasy. My palms and my forehead were sweaty. To make matters worse, my first flight was on a small plane, since the trip was very short. There were less than fifteen people on the plane. During the flight, we experienced a significant amount of turbulence, which certainly did not help to assuage my fears. However, we made it safely to our destination. As we were getting off the plane, I remember hearing someone say, "That was rough. I'm glad I wasn't the pilot for this flight."

My spiritual self recognizes that, ultimately, I am not in charge of my life's flight. Therefore, I don't have to fear because "God is within me." I will admit that is easier said than practiced at times because it is human nature to fear. Yet, knowing that I am not alone and recognizing that God is in charge helps me to feel safer and less worried about all the things that could possibly go wrong.

You are not reading this book by accident or because you had nothing better to do with your time. But it would make no sense for you to read and take seriously all the tips I am offering, but refuse to put them into practice. The time is now. Yes, now, today! You can decide that today is the day you start to soar! Might it be scary? Yes. Soar anyway. Might you wonder if you're making the right decision? Yes. Make the decision anyway. You'll never know just how far you can soar if you keep allowing your fear(s) to hold you hostage. Time is passing you by the longer you wait. The time to soar is NOW! YOU ARE GOOD ENOUGH!

Questions to Ponder

1) How can you start being more patient with yourself today?

2) Using the illustration of the caterpillar, in what stage of development are you today?

3) What are you willing to stop doing right now in order to work on your goals?

4) What is the one thing you are determined to FIGHT for right now?

7
LOVE LIFTED ME

"To fall in love with yourself is the first secret to happiness."
~Robert Morley

I love food! I enjoy sampling new foods and I especially enjoy feasting on some of my favorites: fried chicken, homemade baked macaroni and cheese, cabbage, and hot water cornbread. I'm that guy who takes pictures of every meal I consume in a restaurant and posts them on social media because I want everyone to have the same love and appreciation for food that I have. However, over the past several years, I've gained approximately fifty pounds because of an increase in food consumption and a decrease in exercise. If I'm not committed to making some drastic lifestyle changes, my love for food will eventually lead to health problems and potentially even my demise.

It took a long time for me to realize that food was a crutch for me. Whenever I felt especially stressed, discouraged, frustrated, or otherwise overwhelmed with life, I would start to eat. When I ate for comfort, I never chose the meals that were healthy for me, like fruits and vegetables. I ate the food that would make me feel good for the moment. Little did I recognize at the time, food was becoming a substitute for my lack of self-love and self-esteem.

Oh, don't get me wrong; I am a "professional happy person." In other words, I am that person who can be on the brink of my emotional bridge, but no one would know because I can portray the image of being happy at any given time. One would have to be very close to me to know when things are not going well in my world. I liked keeping myself guarded because it meant I didn't have to suffer the potential ridicule of those who said I wasn't good enough. I felt that if I could "play the part" of being happy, that would get me by just long enough to do what I needed to do in life.

There were many problems with this strategy. For one thing, I am not doing myself any favors by being dishonest with the person who knows me better than anyone else—me! I am doing myself a grave disservice by pretending to be someone I am not. Another problem with this strategy is that pretending to love myself robbed others of the opportunity to demonstrate their genuine love toward me. I believe that vibes are kindred; good vibes connect with other good vibes. But phony vibes also connect with other phony vibes. When I am not true to myself, other people notice, and they are far more hesitant to offer their most authentic selves to me.

I notice this most often in my regular interactions with patients and family members. I have been a hospital chaplain for many years. I notice that when I enter a patient's room and I am "too happy," often the person I am visiting tries to match what they perceive to be my level of happiness. When this happens, they are far less likely to express what is really going on or share their more intimate fears and anxiety. I've matured to a place in my life where I understand that authenticity is borne from a place of genuine self-love.

What love is not

To understand what genuine self-love is, it might be more helpful to define what it is not. First of all, genuine self-love is not perfection. Part of what led to my feelings of low self-esteem and not feeling good enough is because I always felt like I wasn't perfect. I made myself sick, literally, by trying to be perfect. Guess what I learned? I learned that I'm never going to be perfect; neither are you. We were created as human beings with flaws, prone to failure and mistakes. Just because you are not perfect doesn't mean that you don't love yourself.

I have a habit of regularly and consistently telling my daughter that I love her. Even though she is only four years old at this time, I've noticed that she continually seeks my approval for everything. She is also aware of when she has done something wrong. After Halloween this past October, I instructed her to only eat one piece of candy. Of course, I made the mistake of leaving the candy bucket in her bedroom. When I went to read her a bedtime story and put her to sleep, I noticed quite a few candy wrappers on her floor. When I asked her about this, she confessed that she had eaten more than one piece of candy. I told her I was very disappointed and she started crying. I assumed she was crying because she thought she was about to be disciplined. But when I asked why she was crying, her response completely caught me off guard. She said she was crying because she thought I "wasn't going to love her anymore because she had been a bad girl." That was a critical moment in my relationship with my daughter and with myself.

I had to explain to my daughter that even though I was disappointed that she had not followed my instructions, nothing she could ever do would cause me to stop loving her. Yes, she had consequences for her actions (which, in this case, just involved me removing the candy bucket from her room), but my love for her never stopped.

The problem with many of us is that we've not resolved the fact that even though we may fail in different areas of our lives, we don't ever have to stop loving ourselves. For that matter, even when we feel like other people have stopped loving us, whether it is true or not, this should not impact our self-love. I am learning to give myself grace and realize that self-love doesn't have to flutter with the wind. In fact, these days, I'm learning to love myself more because of my failures. Failures help remind me that I am human and that I am not perfect; when I fall, I've learned to love myself even harder.

Love is also not always contingent upon others. I know, you're probably thinking, "But what about babies? If you don't show love to them when they are young, they run the risk of lacking certain social skills." That may be true, but many of us live as though our worth and value is contingent upon the love of others. It's not. Our worth and value is contingent upon our existent on the earth. Period. The fact that we have been created is proof that our Creator thinks we are worthy.

Many people find themselves in failed relationships because they wrongfully assumed they would "find love" in someone else. You can't find something for yourself in someone else. You might appreciate what you believe someone else has, but their self-love is not going to increase your own. You have to work at appreciating who you are independent of the people in your life. If you don't love yourself genuinely and authentically, what makes you think that being with someone else is going to make you love yourself more? It might make you emotionally dependent, but it won't fill the void that only self-love can fill. Only when you are able to own the fact that you are good enough will your internal love vibe connect with your external environment.

Love pains

As I first started writing this section, I thought to myself, "Hmm, love pains. There's an oxymoron." Love is not supposed to be painful, right? Love is supposed to be warm and fuzzy and happy. It is supposed to always smell like a bed of roses and it is always supposed to have access to all the resources that one could possibly need to have a wonderful and remarkable life, right? Well, actually, no. Here's what I mean.

When I was a teenager, I experienced a wide range of physical ailments. Some were related to stress, while others were not. It was especially difficult at the very end of my teen years when I experienced a growth spurt. It seemed that I had continual headaches, accompanied by aches and pains in my joints. After seeing the doctor and specialists to rule out more serious issues, I finally received a diagnosis that I wasn't expecting: growing pains! The doctor explained that as my body went through that growth spurt, I was prone to experience increased aches and pains because my body needed to get used to a new normal. The doctor explained that the pain would eventually go away and that I would likely be taller as a result. (Of course, having leveled off at the gargantuan height of 5'5, I have some questions for that doctor. I knew for sure that with the pains I had experienced, I should have been around 6'4 or taller).

Love follows the same pattern in an ironically curious way. For me to develop a strong sense of self-love, I had to live through the pain of working through my past. I had to endure the suffering of all my addictions that I had substituted in the place of the love that was missing in my life, including comfort food. I had to break myself from the need to depend on other people for validation and affection (which I defined as love at that time in my life). I had to replace my sense of not feeling good enough with affirmations, images, and resolutions that underscored the reality I was seeking.

In general, I don't expect that most of you reading this book are going out looking for pain, but love pains are completely worth the trouble. When I look back over what I went through to become the self-loving, authentic person I believe myself to be today, I am grateful. Pain is typically never easy to endure, but it has its benefits.

When I served in the Air Force, we were required to do physical training at least three times per week. During those years of military service, I was in the best health of my life because the regular cardiovascular and muscle building exercises helped to keep my body in great shape, but I hated doing many of the exercises because I knew I would be sore the next day (and with some exercises, like planks or sit ups, I might be sore for the next week.) But when I look back at pictures from when I suffered through those exercises, I realize that it made a tremendous difference. Going through (and growing through) the love pains process can make that same kind of difference.

Love looks like you

Some years ago when I was a youth pastor, I asked a small group of elementary school students to draw me a picture of what they thought love looked like. I received a variety of different pictures, most of which had some reference to hearts or cupid. Some had references to food ("love is a juicy cheeseburger," for example; you get the point). One particular picture caught my attention because of the student's creativity and wisdom beyond her years. By no means was she an artist, but her picture was a simple stick figure. When the class asked her to explain her image, she said, "This is supposed to be me. Love looks like me." I don't know what happened to that young person; I don't even remember her name. But that image and description has stuck with me to this day.

You see, if I were to ask you to do that same activity, I would imagine I would see any number of responses and images. But in the end, love looks like you. You were uniquely created to co-exist with humans and nature in the world. You don't have to "find" love because you can *be* love; in fact, you *are* love. As you more and more understand yourself to be good enough, you will start to realize that you are the very essence of what love is. You will start to see yourself as worthy of a place in the world, competent, courageous, fearless, and capable of accomplishing anything you want to do or be.

When people look at you, what do they see? No, I'm not talking about the dimples in your cheek or the gap in your teeth. What do they see when they *experience* you? Do they see love? Do they see someone who recognizes their worth? Do they see someone who owns their authentic self, including all the flaws, flops, and failures inherently associated with you? Do they see an unconditional commitment to self-acceptance, understanding that they are not perfect? Do they see a person who keeps trying no matter how often they have to fall and get back up again? If so, when people look at you, they see love.

The other day I was asked to preach the funeral of a woman in my church. The family told me that her favorite Scripture from the Bible was 1 Corinthians 13. I had scanned this Scripture many times over the years, but it wasn't until I had to give her eulogy that one particular section stood out to me: "Love is patient; love is kind; love is not envious or boastful or arrogant or rude. It does not insist on its own way; it is not irritable or resentful; it does not rejoice in wrongdoing, but rejoices in the truth. It bears all things, believes all things, hopes all things, endures all things. Love never ends." (1 Corinthians 13:4-8, NRSV)

Suddenly it hit me. Love is not always about the "other person." These same attributes of love can just as easily apply to us. It's not enough to be patient and kind with others; it's just as important to be patient with and kind to yourself. My favorite part of that quote is that love never ends. Just like my daughter was afraid that I was going to stop loving her because she had done wrong, I've found myself afraid that I was going to stop loving myself because of how I thought others perceived me.

Today, lack of self-love is not an issue for me. Today, I realize that self-love is solely my responsibility. When I love me, others can connect my self-love with their self-love to create a dynamic and fruitful bond. As you move from not enough to good enough, know that you are not only *LOVED*, know that you ARE love!

Questions to Ponder

1) How have you traditionally defined love and how has your definition of love changed after reading this chapter?

2) Who are some of the people that you have been dependent upon to define how much you felt loved in the past? How were they able to maintain such a strong effect on your life?

3) What would a drawing of love look like for you today?

4) What is one change you will make today that will transform the love you have for yourself?

8

GET OUT OF YOUR WAY!

"Self-sabotage is when we say we want something and then go about making sure it doesn't happen."
~Alyce Cornyn-Selby

I have never been a good dancer. While I have been blessed with some sense of rhythm, I have not been blessed with good balance. I am one of the clumsiest people I know. In fact, on the night of my high school prom, I was given the name "Left Feet" because I kept tripping over myself and my date. To make matters worse, sometimes I don't even have to be dancing. I will just be walking down the street and trip over my own feet. (My daughter said to me just the other day, "Daddy, you almost fell because your feet got in the way!") While I am well aware of this physical characteristic, there are also other ways I've managed to get in my own way. This chapter looks at some of the most troublesome barriers I've experienced along my journey toward becoming good enough. As I've already mentioned, making the transition from not enough to good enough is not an easy process; it won't happen overnight. But it is possible!

Procrastination

If one could be paid for procrastination, I would be a millionaire by now! There are many different reasons (or excuses) why people wait as long as possible to make certain changes in their life. Part of the reason it took me so long to write this book is because I waited for years until I felt like I was "ready" to write. I could have had this book written and published years ago, but instead I allowed me to get in my own way, and I waited…and waited. For many of us, procrastination is a well-defined art. We wait until the last minute to do everything, and then we're shocked to discover that we have missed out on some of the potential benefits of getting things done and out of the way.

For example, I've wanted to be an author, a motivational speaker, and a pastor for many years. But I kept putting off opportunities to excel in each of those areas. Sometimes it was out of fear: fear that I would be rejected, fear that I wouldn't be taken seriously, fear of success or failure (see Chapter 2). But, it has been amazing to me to see the way in which doors have opened almost effortlessly when I decided to stop putting off my dreams.

YOU ARE GOOD ENOUGH to do whatever you want to do in life. You have remarkable and tremendous potential for greatness simply because you are alive! But you're selling yourself short because you won't take the necessary action to do what you know you've been called and created to do! Here's the thing about life. Life is not going to force you to be great! Life is also not going to force you to be good enough! You must do the necessary work to show the universe (and, dare I say yourself) that you are capable of pursuing and achieving your greatness.

When I started actively engaging this good enough journey, I realized I was hurting only myself in the long run. All my friends had written books, but I still sat on my great ideas, doing nothing. My friends had become highly sought after motivational speakers in their own right. In fact, in many cases, I was the person who introduced them to individuals who could help them reach that goal. But when it came to me, I kept putting it off. Let's not even talk about how I turned down a good number of senior pastor positions because I didn't feel qualified or ready enough to assume such a sacred and weighty responsibility.

I had no one to blame for my procrastination but me. The same is true for you! You're holding yourself up! Stop it! You're allowing yourself to miss out on some of the best days and times of your life. Stop it! You will never know exactly what you can achieve until you get off of your good ideas and start forming a plan to make them happen. Think about it. What's really holding you back? Fear? You already know you can overcome that. Resources? Bad excuse. There are plenty of resources available and people willing to help you if you ask for it. Money? Money is another poor excuse. Just because you don't have all the money you think you need doesn't mean you shouldn't start somewhere with the few pennies you do have.

When it came to procrastination, I was the master of excuses. It was more emotionally comforting to be the victim than to do the hard work of becoming the captain of my own destiny. As a result, I was only as good as I was active. The more emotionally lazy I allowed myself to become, the less I wanted to engage with my dreams and goals. Some might say, "Well, isn't that a symptom of depression?" Perhaps. But I have learned that depression only has as much power over me as I allow it to have. (Indeed, it is true that clinical depression is a real diagnosis with symptoms that can be controlled through medication, but from a more "big picture" perspective, I have more control over depression than I once allowed myself to believe).

A few years ago, a friend decided she wanted to start a business. When she first mentioned it to me, she was excited and I was so happy for her. She seemed like she was completely committed to starting this business because she said it had been in her heart since she was in her 20s. My friend went to every conference available on starting a business, writing plans, securing resources, etc. She secured a mentor and was focused on reading books about how other entrepreneurs started their businesses.

Over time, I noticed that I would hear about her business aspirations less and less. I knew she had recently given birth, so I assumed this was the result of raising a newborn baby. But when I ran into her at a local coffee shop, she told me she still had the idea. She "has just been putting it off; no reason in particular." I could so relate. And in true friend form, I started to inspire and encourage her to restart her process toward starting the business. Eventually she did. But by the time she started her business, she had missed out on a wonderful opportunity for her target audience because someone else had a similar idea and capitalized on that group. I couldn't be too hard on my friend though, because while I was inspiring her, I still had not even started working toward my goals. Procrastination is an enemy which must be stopped—not eventually, but now!

Negative self-talk

Part of making the transition from not enough to good enough involves being intentional about how you speak about yourself. Clearly, much of my low self-esteem started as the result of what other people were saying about me. But, when I started to embrace the fact that the words, opinions, and thoughts of others don't carry as much weight as my own, I realized that I also needed to make a change. I believe we can literally make ourselves worse by speaking negatively about ourselves and our situation. This is not to say that you are to be unrealistic. Rather, this is to say that just because a situation may look bad, doesn't mean you have to accept "bad" as final.

I'll never forget when I worked for the Division of Family and Children Services in my state. I had a teenager on my foster care caseload who, upon our first introduction, said, "I just want you to know that I'm bipolar and I have ADHD (attention deficit hyperactivity disorder)." This teenager used this diagnosis whenever he met with someone new as a way to explain away his behavioral challenges. What I found curious was that I could never find written documentation of his diagnoses. When I eventually met his biological mother, I asked about his psychological history and treatment. The mother laughed and said, "There's nothing wrong with him. He just heard somebody say that he would *probably* end up having those conditions one day because they run in our family." When I asked the young man about this, he confirmed that what his mother said was true. He told me, "They already said I was going to probably have it anyway, so I figured I would just let people know ahead of time."

Ok, so first, it's not ok to tell people you have a diagnosis when you don't; let's be clear about that. But second, from that conversation, we made a pact that he would never use those terms to describe himself anymore. Rather, he would use positive, affirming words to describe himself to others. For example, he would say, "I'm getting better every day. I'm blessed. I'm intelligent. I'm capable of doing whatever I set my mind to do." Within just a few months, I witnessed a tremendous transformation in this young man's behavior all because he modified his negative self-talk and started to say positive things about himself.

Understanding that you are good enough involves speaking positively about yourself. If you're anything like me, occasionally you have those moments when you don't feel your best. Maybe you don't feel attractive, or you don't feel confident in a given scenario. I've learned how to start speaking positively even when I don't see what I'm saying. This all started after an activity I learned when I attended a conference. The conference facilitator encouraged all of us to write on index cards the things that we wanted to be true about us. On my cards, I wrote down things like, "I am confident. I am courageous. I am handsome. I am articulate. I am good enough." We were then told to post the index cards around the mirror in our bathroom. Whenever we saw the card, we were to speak out loud the affirmation on the card.

At first, I thought that was the silliest activity, especially the first thing in the morning. (I'm not a morning person, and I certainly don't feel most of those attributes when I first wake up). Yet, I started the project and continued with it for quite some time. Over time, I noticed I had more of a "pep in my step." I started to feel more confident, handsome, courageous, and articulate. What's more, other people started to compliment me on the very attributes I had been affirming. (Remember how I said that your energy will connect with the energy of others? This is a good example of that in action). As you affirm the positive, you start to embody the positive. The same is true for the negative. So it is always in your best interest to avoid negative self-talk.

Part of avoiding negative self-talk also involves not holding on to negative thoughts. I've sat through many meditation exercises during which the leader said, "When a thought comes to your mind, let it go so that your mind can be free." What a liberating exercise! To get to a place of believing that YOU ARE GOOD ENOUGH, you must not only speak it but also block out all the negative noises that tell you otherwise.

Comparing apples to oranges

A few years ago, I decided to trade in my car. As part of that long process of searching for the perfect vehicle, I test drove every type of vehicle that I was interested in. Eventually, I decided that I wanted a BMW-7 series vehicle. Unfortunately, at that time, the BMW was not in my budget, but I test drove it anyway. It felt like I was driving on a cloud. The car was fast, it was powerful, it was quiet. It was everything I wanted in a vehicle and everything I had come to expect in a BMW. When the test drive was over, I knew I couldn't afford it at that time, so I sadly went down the street to the Honda dealership. Hondas are great vehicles. I've driven one for years. But, Hondas are not BMWs. No matter how I tried to "gun it" (speed up) during the test drive, it just didn't perform as well as the BMW. Why? Because it's not a BMW, bummer. Even though I have now been blessed to afford the BMW of my dreams, I've become quite comfortable and, more importantly, content driving the Honda. (The Honda is also much cheaper to repair, and the gas is less expensive).

In life, many of us self-destruct and minimize our worth because we are comparing ourselves to other people. We see someone else doing what we aspire to do, and suddenly we get discouraged because we perceive that they're doing "big things" and we are not. They've already written nine books and you haven't started one. They've already started their business and you don't even know what you want to do. They've already been in a magazine while you're still just reading the cover of the magazine in the checkout line. Here are a few things to remember.

First of all, "everything that glitters is not gold." I learned that expression from my grandmother. Just because you see someone else with something doesn't mean it's as good as it looks. For that matter, just because you see someone with a smile on their face, doesn't mean that they have already conquered the self-esteem issues you may still have. Second, everyone has a process they must go through to get what they want out of life. Just because you've made an intentional commitment to recognizing that you ARE GOOD ENOUGH doesn't mean you're going to look like someone else who has had great self-esteem for many years!

Furthermore, you have to be ok with who you are. You have to own where you are in your process and realize that eventually you will get where you're trying to be. But never, never, never compare yourself with someone else. It's always good to aspire to greatness. You might identify greatness in someone else. But if you try to be THEM, you will never succeed at being authentically YOU. Be yourself! Good enough looks very different for everyone. It's up to you to decide what good enough looks like for you.

I started this book telling you about my interaction with Simone. I would like to hope that she left my office that day with a clear vision of what she wanted to do, along with feeling empowered to start the process to apply for nursing school. She owes it to herself to follow her dream, her true dream, not one that had been carved out for her. But she inspired me that day to follow one of my dreams, which has been writing this book. She inspired me that day to remind myself that I AM GOOD ENOUGH to do whatever I want to do.

YOU ARE GOOD ENOUGH too! No more excuses! No more negative energy! No more low self-esteem! No more self-defeating statements! You have been created at this time to fulfill a certain purpose in life. Everything that you need to get started is already within you. FIGHT for what you want! FIGHT for what you see! FIGHT for what you know you are capable of achieving! FIGHT until you are able to break through your shell and, until your last breath, FIGHT your way through, from not enough to good enough!

Questions to Ponder

1) How do you get in your own way of accomplishing your dreams?

2) What are some of the triggers that make you retreat into procrastination rather than regularly moving toward your goal?

3) What are some of the things you need to STOP saying about yourself because they are hindering your progress?

4) What positive affirmations will you write and commit to saying about yourself every day?

5) Who are three specific people that you aspire to be like and why?

ABOUT THE AUTHOR

Damion S. Hutchins was adopted at a young age and raised in Warrensville Heights, Ohio. He joined the US Air Force and later pursued a career as a clinical chaplain, motivational speaker, and pastor. Damion received his bachelor's degree in social psychology from Park University and his master of divinity degree in psychology of religion and pastoral care from the Interdenominational Theological Center in Atlanta, Georgia. He serves as the senior pastor of Friendship Baptist Church in Toccoa, Georgia, and is a board-certified clinical chaplain. He is a devoted husband and proud father of one daughter. He and his family live in metropolitan Atlanta, GA.

For more information please visit:

http://www.damionhutchins.com.